DISNEY'S

12 | WONDERFUL WORLD OF KNOWLEDGE

Disney's
Wonderful
World of
Knowledge

THE DANBURY PRESS

THE DANBURY PRESS

a division of Grolier Enterprises, Inc.

ROBERT B. CLARKE	*Publisher*
ROBERT G. BARTNER	*Marketing Director*
GILBERT EVANS	*Creative Director*
THE STONEHOUSE PRESS	*Production Supervision*

ARNOLDO MONDADORI EDITORE

MARIO GENTILINI	*Editor-in-Chief*
ELISA PENNA	*Supervising Editor*
GIOVAN BATTISTA CARPI CLAUDIO MAZZOLI	*Illustrators*
GUIDO MARTINA	*Author*

"Disney's WONDERFUL WORLD OF KNOWLEDGE"
is an updated and enlarged English version of
an encyclopedia heretofore printed in the Italian language by
ARNOLDO MONDADORI EDITORE, MILAN
and entitled (in English Translation) "Disney ENCYCLOPEDIA"

CONTENTS

ONCE UPON A TIME

Our adventure-filled journey across the past, present, and future is continuing at top speed, girls and boys. And who gets the honor of guiding you on this stretch of your journey? It's yours truly, known all over the world and surrounding areas as Goofy!

This part of our tour is filled with old tales, new tales, fanciful tales, and some jokes. Facts or fancies, they add up to fun for everyone.

I am the perfect leader for your trek because my ancestors from way, way back have handed down a huge collection of papers—memoirs, diaries, newspapers, maps—even bills, wills, and contracts—all yellow with age. They are in a big trunk up in my attic at home. Every once in a while I go up and rummage around in them. I pore over them and learn from them, and little by little I have become the Goofy Encyclopedia!

Early in the earth's history molten lava erupted from volcanoes more frequently than it does now. When man came on the scene and saw fire coming out of mountains, he though it might be the work of a god.

FAMILY HISTORY

My great, great, great, great grandfathers! What a bunch, boys and girls! And the greatest was Goofus Poplar Troglodytus, known as Poplar. He got that name from living on a poplar branch. Later he moved down into a cave, and then he got his last name, Troglodytus. You see, the word "troglodyte" comes from the Greek words for "someone who enters a cave."

I can't tell you Grandfather Poplar's exact birthday because he lived long, long before people had begun to keep records. In Poplar's day there was no ink, no paper, and, in fact, no writing! The wonderful convenience known as writing and the tools people use to write with did not come until much later. The Sumerians, Egyptians, Chinese, and others developed writing about 3,000 or 4,000 years before the birth of Christ.

After the invention of writing, people began to leave written information behind—everything from shopping lists to descriptions of military campaigns. With writing, the history of the human race

During the age of the dinosaurs, or giant reptiles, the earth may possibly have looked like the pictures shown above and below. Although science fiction stories and films sometimes show prehistoric people living side by side with dinosaurs, this was not the case. Creatures such as dinosaurs and pterodactyls became extinct (died out) at least 100,000,000 years before early manlike creatures made their appearance.

began! The time before people could write is called prehistory.

OK, boys and girls, let's go back into prehistory and see what life was like when Grandpa Poplar lived in his tree and why he left it when he did. First, I want you to understand that Grandpa Poplar and his relatives were very, very distant ancestors of man. They lived some 20,000,000 years ago! They weren't very much like man at all—though they were primates. That's the family that man, the apes, and monkeys all belong to. Now, instead of thinking of the real tree Poplar lived in, think of a kind of chart called a "family tree." Then imagine the different parts of the primate family living on different "branches" of that tree. Grandpa Poplar, a monkeylike creature who was someday going to become man, lived on a particular branch of that tree. The other primates also each inhabited a special "branch."

Now back to Grandpa's real life in the trees. He and his relatives spent their day picking fruit from the other trees in the forest and robbing birds' nests of their eggs and baby birds. Life was fairly easy

11

Above, left: The papyrus plant, from which the Egyptians made the first paperlike writing material. The plant's stalk was cut into thin strips, which were then woven together and moistened. Above: An Egyptian lotus. This plant and the papyrus both grow in the shallow part of the Nile and are symbols of the river.

because Grandpa and his friends had nothing to fear except snakes and falling out of trees.

Then something—perhaps a drought—made the forest grow smaller, and Grandpa Poplar could not find enough of his usual food. Down out of the trees he climbed and went looking for food on the open ground—often a grassland—beyond the forest's rim. Here he feasted on moles and ground squirrels, which he dug out of their burrows. Later he became a hunter and chased the antelope and other hoofed mammals of the plains. We think that's why he first stood up on his hind legs—to see his prey over the top of the tall grass.

Standing and walking upright was one of the special things that made Grandpa's relatives develop into man. Another special trait was talking. Talking helped man pass on his knowledge and skills—such as toolmaking—to his sons and grandsons. Talking and thinking went together after man's brain developed. But something you may not know is that man's ability to talk is connected with his having lived in the trees. You'll notice that creatures such as birds and primates that live in the safety of the trees are the animal kingdom's chatterers. Animals that have always lived on the ground tend to be quieter so their enemies cannot find them.

Our ancestors talked and talked. Then ages and ages later (around 3,000 B.C. or earlier), writing, and with it history, began. Writing is a way of capturing words so that they last. First, people captured them by using a picture to stand for an idea. Then—and this was a big step—they made a picture stand for a sound in the spoken language. In each of the places where writing started—Egypt, Sumeria, Babylonia, China, and among the Maya Indians—the writing tools used were those most easily available in the region. In Egypt people wrote with reed pens on sheets made from the papyrus plant. Just notice how much like the word "papyrus" our word "paper" is!

Well, boys and girls, one word has led to another—the spoken to the written—and we have jumped way ahead of our story. Let's go back to Grandpa Poplar. When we left him he was still standing on his hind legs on a grassy plain looking for food and, incidentally, a safe and comfortable place to stay at night.

Grandpa at last found a cave, under a ledge of rock at the plain's edge. Then he began to wonder how to keep warm when it was chilly and how to keep wild animals away. Well, many thousands of

Antoine Lavoisier, the French chemist who explained fire. People learned how to make fire in prehistoric times. But no one knew exactly what happens when burning takes place until Lavoisier made his studies in the 18th century. The English scientist Joseph Priestley had discovered a gas that helped make things burn. Lavoisier explained that fire is the rapid combination of this gas—which he called oxygen—with a fuel.

13

Above: A ziggurat, or terraced shrine, built by the Sumerians. We know these artificial hills enclosing temples were sacred because in the Sumerian writing system the word "sanctuary" (which means a sacred place) is represented by a picture of a house on a mountain.
Opposite page: Decorative panels from the royal tombs of the ancient Sumerian city of Ur. The panels, which are now in the British Museum, show troops and war chariots on parade.

years passed and Grandpa's grandsons developed into creatures somewhat like men before they figured out that what they needed in the cave for warmth and safety was—you guessed it—fire!

FIRE, FIRE!

Our great, great, great, great, grandfathers didn't know what fire was. But when they saw it erupting from craters of volcanoes or bursting from branches hit by lightning, they thought it was something magical. Fire was useful, but it was also terribly destructive. Our ancestors began to ask themselves just what was this mysterious thing that could appear so suddenly with such flaming, terrifying power. They thought it was probably created by some invisible being who lived high up in the sky or far down in the depths of the earth. This being certainly couldn't be a man, so he must be something more than a man—something to be worshiped. And this may be how the first idea of divinity (a god or gods) was born. Fire might be the work of a god or it might be the god himself. As such, fire was sacred. Even today some primitive peoples still think it is wrong to burn impure objects, or to spit into the flames!

There are many legends about how fire first appeared on earth. In an ancient Persian tale a hero named Hushang tried to kill a snake by throwing it against a magic stone. The snake slithered away unharmed, but the stone bounced and hit a rock. The Persian poet Firdausi, retelling this tale, wrote that then a light leaped forth from the rock, the heart of the rock exploded in brilliant flames, and fire was seen for the first time in the world.

According to a North American In-

Above: Greek soldiers, hidden inside the Trojan horse, conquered the city of Troy during the legendary Trojan War.
Opposite page: Ruins of Persepolis, once the capital of ancient Persia (now Iran).

dian legend, a bison gave fire to man. One night, as the bison was galloping across the plains, its hooves hit some stones and sparks flew up. The prairie brush caught fire from the sparks, and soon flames were leaping wildly all about.

It should be clear from these legends that someone discovered the principle on which fire is produced. How had he figured this out? Very simple. One day an alert fellow—much like me—was rubbing two stones together to see which would make the harder tool. The friction (rubbing) between the two stones made sparks that lit the dry grass nearby. Just by chance the man had chosen a piece of flint and a stone containing iron pyrite for his experiment, and that's how lighters were invented!

Other ways to make a spark were to rub two dry sticks together or to twirl a sharpened dry twig very rapidly in a hollowed-out stone. If the friction made enough heat and wood dust, a spark might result.

16

FRIEND AND ENEMY

Though fire became a great friend—keeping people warm, cooking their meals, making their machinery go—it

could also be a fierce and cruel enemy. History is full of stories of terrible fires.

One of the earliest great fires burned down ancient Troy at the end of the Trojan War. The Greeks, who were fighting the Trojans, pretended to give up the fight and leave. But before they left, they placed a huge wooden horse just outside Troy's gates. The Trojans, curious about the gift, opened the gates and dragged the horse inside. That was their biggest mistake, boys and girls, because the horse was hollow and Greek soldiers were hiding inside! That night, while the Trojans slept, the Greeks crept out and took the city. After looting Troy, they burned it to the ground. From the Trojans' mistake in accepting the horse and its disastrous result comes a famous saying: Beware of Greeks bearing gifts!

Another famous fire that did a lot of damage took place during the campaigns of the Greek conqueror Alexander the Great. Having captured the city of Persepolis in Persia, Alexander gave a banquet in the city's vast imperial palace. The story goes that one of the dinner guests, a Greek lady named Thais, suggested that the merrymakers burn down the palace—just for fun! Alexander ordered his soldiers to carry out the whim of his beautiful guest. That's the story—one we are not sure is true—of how the palace of the kings of Persia burned to ashes. Its stone foundations and stately columns, however, can still be seen to this day.

The worst book burning of all time took place in Alexandria, Egypt, in 47 B.C. At that time Alexandria was the greatest center of learning in the world. It had a huge library containing most of the Western world's great books and manuscripts. A Roman army, under the command of Julius Caesar, occupied the

Moscow burning during its occupation by Napoleon's army. As the French army advanced toward Moscow in 1812, the people moved out, leaving Moscow empty. Though the origin of the fire is not known, the Russians probably set

city. The Romans ordered the library and its over 700,000 books and manuscripts burned. A story is told—though it cannot be proven—that for 4 months the waters of Alexandria's 4,000 public baths were heated by fires destroying the priceless volumes.

Maybe the name Pudding Lane sounds funny to you, but it wasn't funny to Londoners in September, 1666. That's the street near London Bridge where the Great Fire of London broke out. It

*the fire to make life hard for the French army.
The fire burned for a number of days during
the middle of September, and much of the wooden
city, including the grain warehouses, burned.
Napoleon's army retreated from Moscow soon
after the fire.*

started in a bakery, and it baked a large part of the old city of London. Samuel Pepys, who kept a now-famous diary, spoke of a "horrid, malicious, bloody flame" that lit up the sky. The fire raged for 4 days and destroyed 13,200 houses, 89 churches, and St. Paul's Cathedral. The St. Paul's Cathedral we see pictures of today is the "new" St. Paul's. It was built between 1675 and 1710 by the architect Sir Christopher Wren to replace the one burnt down in the fire.

THE HOMES OF MAN

We'll never know exactly when early man decided to move from a cave to a house—but we do know why he moved. Caves were dark and damp places, but that wasn't the only reason why man sought a different type of shelter. As our early ancestors slowly discovered more and more about the world around them, they learned how to make tools, raise crops of wheat and barley, and tame wild animals. Gradually there began to develop a different way of life.

Instead of roaming all over the land, early man decided to stay in one place and to tend his garden and animals. But first he needed a shelter to protect his family from bad weather, wild animals, and unfriendly neighbors. Using the materials around him, such as wood, stone, grass, and even mud, man was able to build a "house." Of course it wasn't very fancy or comfortable. But it was home for the people who lived on our earth thousands of years ago.

One house after another was built. Soon small villages were popping up

Large, crowded cities have taken over a great part of the world. But there are still areas of wilderness that have been left practically untouched by human hands.

throughout the countryside. Most of the villages were situated along the banks of rivers, lakes, and streams. Since early man had to grow his own food—there were no supermarkets way back then, you know—the streams provided water for his crops. Streams were also a good source of food because the waters were filled with fish, and what a tasty meal they made!

Since many early houses were located so close to the water's edge, they were built on stilts for protection against possible floods. These houses were so popular, that when man moved to areas where there was no water close by, he still built his home on stilts.

Only remnants of these stilt villages exist in Europe today. However, if we were to travel in some countries of Africa and South America—among other places—we would see picturesque stilt villages, much as they appeared thousands of years ago.

FROM HUTS TO SKYSCRAPERS

Girls and boys, you may not have heard that some of the most unusual 21

Above: There are always many legends about every ancient castle. The Castel dell'Ovo (the Egg Castle), on an island in the Bay of Naples, is no exception. It is said that centuries ago an egg was placed inside a glass that was hung in a room in the castle. When the egg broke, the castle was supposed to fall. That's exactly what happened during the 1300's. The castle was later rebuilt by Queen Joan I of Naples. Right: The sword, spurs, and coat of arms of an Italian nobleman.

houses ever built by man were once found in great numbers throughout the United States. They belonged to the Indians—the first inhabitants of the North American continent. Let's take a quick look at a few of the different kinds of homes they occupied. I have it on very good authority that every Indian tribe built some form of dwelling, and some tribes used more than one type of house. It all depended on the season of the year and the materials that were handy at the time they were building. During the hunting season the Indian was always on

the move in search of bison. So he built a movable house. This portable shelter is called a tepee—as if you didn't know! A tepee is a tall cone-shaped tent of buffalo skins stretched over long, thin poles set in a circle. Some tribes covered their tepees with bark or grass instead of animal skins.

In the spring and autumn, a number of Indian tribes lived in hogans—large earth-covered lodges that, grouped together, formed a village. Actually these lodges were sometimes little more than fancy tepees. The hogan had a framework of

22

heavy poles, with a small hall or passage at the entrance. The poles were covered with a thick layer of earth rather than skins or bark.

The early Indian tribes built houses according to the climate in which they lived. For example, in the northern and mountainous regions of America, the houses had strong walls made of wood, bark, thatch, or reeds. They had to be sturdy enough to keep the snow, wind, and chill out—and the warmth in. In the southern areas, where the climate was much warmer, the houses often had no walls at all. A roof supported by four or six poles did the job.

We can also thank the Indians—the Salado Indians, to be exact—for building America's first skyscraper! Sometime between A.D. 1300 and 1400, members of the Salado tribe built a four-story, 40-foot

adobe tower in southern Arizona. It was used as a watchtower and fort. The first European to visit this unusual construction was a Jesuit missionary, Father Eusebio Francisco Kino, in 1694. He described the tower as being as large as a castle, and named it "the Casa Grande" or "Great House." If we were to place it next to our skyscrapers of today, the Casa Grande Tower would not seem very large, but for its day, it was quite a tall structure.

A HOME FIT FOR A KING

Yes indeed, boys and girls, America has its modern skyscrapers—those immense structures that reach up to brush the clouds. But Europe and Asia have buildings that can't be found in a young nation like the United States—ancient

During medieval times villagers gathered inside castle walls in times of danger. The lord of the manor, to protect his domain, marched his armies to nearby fields where they battled the enemy.

24

castles and huge palaces—all rich in history, glory, and legend.

During the Middle Ages castles were built throughout Europe as fortified homes for local lords. As the centuries passed the castles, though a bit damp and drafty, were turned into splendid homes for kings and noblemen.

How about coming along with old Goofy to visit historic Windsor Castle, located just outside of London. This centuries-old fortress is an official residence of British kings and queens. The first building on the site was a wooden stockade built by William the Conqueror sometime around 1070. Through the years British monarchs have added to the original structure. Today, Windsor Castle stands as a home fit for a king . . . or a queen.

While we're in the neighborhood, let's fly across the English Channel and travel through France. There are two palaces that I want you to see. The Palace of Versailles, just outside of Paris, has often been called the most beautiful royal palace in the world, and for good reason. It was designed and built in the 17th

Left: Grass houses of the Wichita tribe constructed in "Indian City," Oklahoma.
Above: A portion of the rear facade of the Palace of Versailles. This royal residence of French kings contains hundreds of rooms, including the famous Hall of Mirrors. The palace sits among formal gardens, lawns, walks, and elaborate fountains and lakes.

century for Louis XIV, king of France. Its formal gardens, lakes, fountains, and private and state apartments are famous all over the world. In 1837 the Palace of Versailles became a national monument and museum.

Also on the outskirts of Paris we'll find Fontainebleau Palace, once used as a summer residence for many French kings. And, believe it or not, in past years Fontainebleau was also used as a prison. Pope Pius VII was held captive there by Napoleon I from 1812 to 1814. I suppose if you have to spend some time in prison, Fontainebleau is just the place!

THE PALACE OF SANS SOUCI

Are you as dog tired as I am at the end of a day? I've often thought it would be pleasant to have a cottage by the sea . . . a nice little place where one could relax with a bowl of chopped meat in front of a roaring fireplace. Well, believe me, girls and boys, we common people—and dogs

Opposite page: The famous horseshoe-shaped staircase of Fontainebleau Palace.

Above: In this beautiful room of Sans Souci Palace, Johann Sebastian Bach played the piano for King Frederick II.

—aren't the only ones who feel that way. What's good for us is good for kings as well. Take King Frederick II of Prussia, for example. In days gone by Prussia occupied part of what is now East Germany. But getting back to Frederick the Great, or King Fred, as I always called him . . . he, too, liked to relax and get away from the affairs of state. In 1744 he commissioned a palace to be built at Potsdam, Germany. When it was completed in 1747, Frederick named the one-story high palace, Sans Souci, which is French for "carefree."

29

King Frederick invited all of his friends to stay at Sans Souci while they were in town, and many of them did. Among his famous guests were the French writer, Voltaire, and Johann Sebastian Bach, the German composer. Visitors to Sans Souci enjoyed browsing through the palace's library, strolling around the beautiful grounds, and looking at the many paintings done by some of the world's greatest artists. It was quite a weekend retreat.

TREASURE TROVES

Speaking of comfortable homes, we can't just pass by Buckingham and Blenheim palaces without paying a visit. After all, these are probably two of the most famous treasure troves in all the world. So it's back to London! And if we're lucky, we'll see the queen.

Since 1837 the British royal family has made its London home in Buckingham Palace. This stately building sits among 40 acres of beautiful gardens. If we walk through the many rooms of the palace— the Picture Gallery and the Throne Room, among others—we'll see one of the world's finest art collections. And, of course, we can't miss the changing of the palace guards. This colorful ceremony takes place every morning—rain or shine —and I promised Minnie Mouse I'd take a picture of the guards.

Blenheim Palace, located near Oxford, was built for the first duke of Marlborough by Queen Anne of England in the early 1700's. I don't know about you, but I wouldn't mind spending a month or two living at Blenheim. The palace, aside from being the birthplace of Sir Winston Churchill, is just filled with history. Its many great halls and large rooms contain an outstanding collection of paintings,

Above: It is rumored that Diogenes, the 4th-century B.C. Greek philosopher, lived in a wooden tub. Here he is seen talking with Alexander the Great, the powerful general.

The magnificent Castel Sant' Angelo lies on the banks of the Tiber River in Rome, Italy.

tapestries, furniture, and china. Yes sir, an absolute treasure trove if ever I saw one!

FAMOUS CASTLES

Our day would not be complete if we didn't do a little extra castle hopping. And the best place to do this is merry old England, of course! Stay close together because we just might run into a few . . . er . . . well, you know . . . ghosts! What's a wonderful old castle without a ghost or two?

Our first stop is Colchester Castle. This ancient structure was built by the early French invaders, the Normans, in about 1080. In order to build the castle, the Normans had to use materials taken from even earlier Roman constructions.

We'll need bathing suits and maybe waterwings, or even a raft, if we're going to visit Bodiam Castle in Sussex, England. That's because we have to swim across a moat. A moat is a water-filled ditch that surrounds a castle. In the olden days these deep waters made it difficult for attackers to reach the castle walls. In fact, the only approach to Bodiam Castle was a wooden bridge over the moat.

One of the most beautiful of the English castles is Warwick, which was built in the 14th century. One of its towers, however, dates from shortly after the Norman Conquest of England in 1066. The castle, which is still the home of the Earls of Warwick, contains many valuable works of art. Of all the castle's treasures, I particularly like the collection of suits of armor.

31

PALACES FOR THE DEAD

Thousands of years ago, V.I.P.'s—very important people—weren't content just living in luxurious surroundings. They wanted their life after death to be equally as elegant. The Egyptian pharaoh Khufu, better known as Cheops, ordered a great pyramid to be built at Giza. This was to be his tomb. He wanted all of his worldly possessions to be buried with his body. Cheops wished to enter his new life in the lap of luxury!

In Halicarnassus, Asia Minor (present-day Turkey), Queen Artemisia built a great marble tomb for her husband, King Mausolus. Of course, all this happened a long, long time ago . . . about 350 B.C. to be exact. The monument was so beautiful that the word "mausoleum" became part of our language and has come to mean a magnificent tomb. Unfortunately, only a few fragments of the tomb remain. Both the Great Pyramid at Giza and the Mausoleum at Halicarnassus were two of the Seven Wonders of the Ancient World.

The Roman emperor Hadrian began construction of his tomb, the Castel Sant' Angelo on the banks of the Tiber River in A.D. 135. I'll bet he had no idea that his final resting place would later be used as a fort, a prison, and a refuge for popes in times of danger.

THE JEWEL OF INDIA

Hold onto old Goofy's tail, boys and girls, because we're off to visit the most famous tomb of them all. With one giant leap we've landed in India, right in front of the Taj Mahal. This magnificent tomb has been called the most beautiful building in the world and for good reason. Whoa—I'm getting ahead of my story.

First, let me give you a short history lesson.

Back in 1632, Shah Jahan, an emperor in northern India, decided to build the Taj Mahal as a memorial to his wife, Mumtaz Mahal, who had just died. Shah Jahan searched all of Asia for the best architects. It is believed that Ustad Isa, a Persian, was chosen to design the mausoleum.

It took more than 20 years and the labors of 20,000 workmen to complete the Taj Mahal. Shah Jahan was greatly pleased with the large graceful building of pure white marble. In fact, he thought so highly of the mausoleum that he took steps to see that no building would ever equal its beauty. It is said that Shah Jahan had the architect blinded so that he could

The majestic Taj Mahal stands at the end of a long reflecting pool. The tomb, located at Agra, India, was built by Shah Jahan as a memorial to his beloved wife.

PERIWINKLE

HYACINTH

SPEEDWELL

CORNFLOWER

CUCKOOFLOWER

Before Botticelli painted Primabera, he must have spent hours studying the flowers that appear so beautifully in his work. On the facing page there is a part of the painting with squares showing the parts enlarged on this page and on page 37. The photograph from top to bottom shows three of these flowers: periwinkle, corn flowers, and violets.

never again create anything as beautiful as the Taj Mahal. This may not be true, but it is one of the many legends that surround the great mausoleum.

The Taj Mahal, which contains the tombs of Shah Jahan and his wife, stands on a large white marble terrace. The mausoleum, with its gleaming white domes and slender minarets, is reflected in a nearby pool. Beautiful gardens with shrubs and dark green cypress trees surround the building.

There's no question that the Taj Mahal is quite a place. For that matter, so are all of the castles, palaces and . . . er . . .

tombs that we've visited. But for me, there's no finer home in all the world than my little cottage in Duckburg.

IN AN ARTIST'S GARDEN

You may wonder how your old pal Goofy got to have so many facts packed between his long ears. I'll let you in on the secret. It was by looking hard at the things around me. This painting by an Italian artist, Botticelli, is called *Primavera* ("Spring"). It is full of beautiful flowers. Look closely at the painting and see how many of them you can find.

35

At least 40 kinds of flowers are in Primavera. Some grew only in the artist's mind. Others (above), such as the coltsfoot, daisy, and Christmas Rose, are real. On the opposite page there is an enlargement of the flowery lawn in the painting showing a number of lovely blossoms.

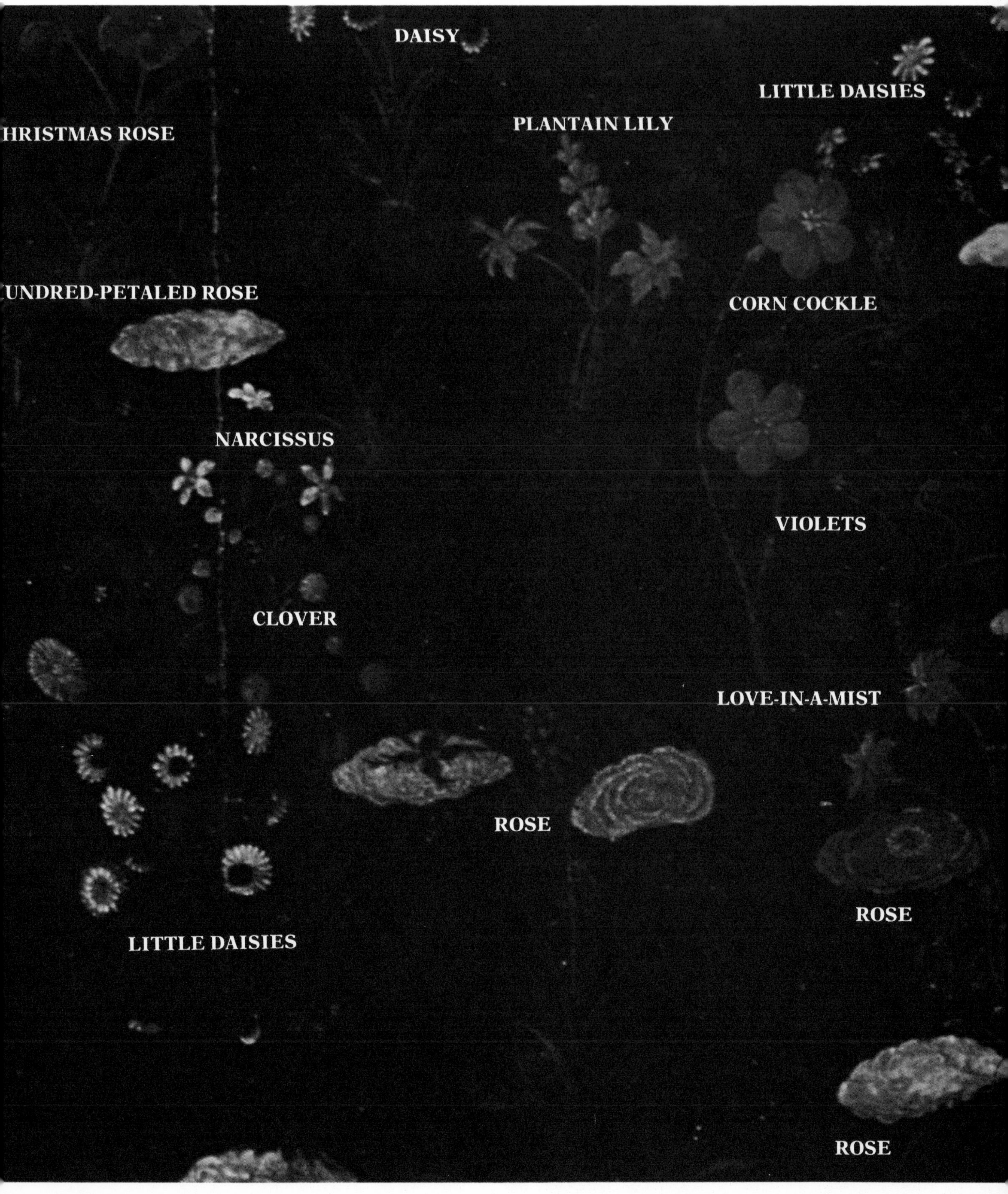

DAISY

LITTLE DAISIES

CHRISTMAS ROSE

PLANTAIN LILY

HUNDRED-PETALED ROSE

CORN COCKLE

NARCISSUS

VIOLETS

CLOVER

LOVE-IN-A-MIST

ROSE

ROSE

LITTLE DAISIES

ROSE

MAN'S BEST FRIENDS

Let's talk about a new subject, my friends. How about taking a look at some of your animal friends like—well, why not?—me, Goofy. If you let me start out by talking about man's best friends—dogs —I promise that I'll tell you something about the other members of the animal kingdom later on. O.K.?

It may not sound exactly modest but there are lots of reasons why dogs are called man's best friends in the animal world. They are brave, loyal, and helpful. Since the earliest days men have trusted dogs to guard their children, their homes, and other animals. Dogs are also among the oldest of man's animal friends. I mean that dogs—or their ancestors— were among the first animals man made into household pets and helpers.

Speaking of ancestors, they say that I, Goofy, and all dogs are descended from a small weasel-like animal called Miacis who lived about 40,000,000 years ago. That's right—40,000,000 years ago—if you can imagine such a long time, which

According to the English writer Jerome K. Jerome, "A dog never bothers asking you if you're right or wrong; he doesn't care at all if you're rich or poor, ignorant or learned, sinner or saint; you are his friend and that's enough."

I have trouble doing. Wow, all I can say is that is a long, long, long time.

Not quite so long ago—approximately 15,000,000 years ago—my next ancestor appeared on the scene. His name was Tomarctus and he not only looked a lot like a wolf but was their ancestor, too. In fact, all dogs are related to three familiar wild animals—the wolf, the coyote, and the jackal. Our distant cousins are the raccoons, foxes, and bears.

Now that you have gotten an idea of how long dogs have been around and what a big complicated family tree we have, we can look at some of the more modern dogs.

DOGS OF YESTERDAY AND TODAY

They tell me that it was in the New Stone Age that men first began to tame and train dogs to go hunting with them and to work as watchdogs. The next step was for men to settle in one place and raise sheep and cattle. Dogs settled down and were trained to guard the flocks, as sheepdogs still do.

Paintings and drawings that have come down to us from ancient times show that

39

Above: The French poodle comes in three sizes: toy, miniature, and standard. The poodle spends quite a bit of time at the "hair dresser" being clipped for high fashion.

Opposite page: These frisky puppies will grow up to be working dogs. Some of them will be used to pull sleds through the snows of the north country.

the Egyptians and the Assyrians kept dogs as pets. They say that the Egyptian house dog is the forerunner of three kinds of modern dogs—the pug, the Pekingese, and the poodle. The tall, graceful Saluki was bred in Egypt, too, and is now known as the oldest recognized breed of dog.

Another very ancient breed of dog is the Samoyed who comes from the far north. Samoyeds, whose long furry coats protected them from the bitter northern winters, are related to some of the greatest hunting dogs such as the setters, pointers, and spaniels.

You are probably getting the idea that the dog world is very large and you are right! To make matters a little simpler dogs are usually divided into big groups depending on the dog's special skills.

40

There are six of these groups—sporting dogs, hounds, working dogs, terriers, toy dogs, and non-sporting dogs.

The sporting group includes the dogs that are good hunters like pointers, set-ters, and spaniels. Hounds such as bassets, dachshunds, elkhounds, and whippets were bred to hunt fur-bearing animals. Working dogs like boxers, German shep-herds, huskies, and Doberman pinschers

Above: The Norwich terrier. Terrier breeds were developed almost entirely in the British Isles and Ireland.

really do work helping policemen, Eskimos, and firemen among many others. Terriers were originally bred because they were so good at catching rats and other rodents. The toy dogs make a big beast like me laugh, but some of them—like toy poodles, chihuahuas, and Yorkshire terriers—are nice when you get to know them. The sixth group—the non-sporting dogs—used to be raised to work but now are just house pets. Among this group is the intelligent standard poodle —the one that gets such fancy haircuts.

O.K.! I know, I promised. Now we'll take a look at other animals besides dogs!

Right: Basset hounds are known for their sad eyes, long ears, and droopy faces.

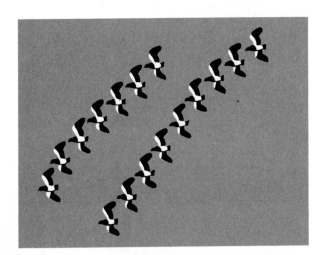

BIRDS, BIRDS, BIRDS

As you can see I, Goofy, have some pals among our feathered friends—the birds. They have even let me in on some secrets about their lives and I'll share them with you now.

Nearly all birds, they tell me, have a kind of calendar that they follow each year. Each spring adult birds choose mates, and they build nests for their eggs. When the baby birds hatch out of their eggs they are fed by their parents and taught how to care for themselves.

In the fall many birds fill their bodies with food to get ready for the trip to their winter homes. In the fall you often see swarms of birds heading to warm places. In spring these traveling or migratory birds head north again to their summer homes. When the birds build new nests in a tree or bush near where you live, you can be sure the last snow has fallen, the last icicle has melted, and that spring has come.

Migrating birds often appear to be flying in formation like airplanes. The good order of their flying is reflected in the fact that they fly along definite travel routes each year. These routes are called flyways. There are at least seven important flyways across North America. But the distance birds travel when they migrate varies from only a few miles to thousands of miles.

44

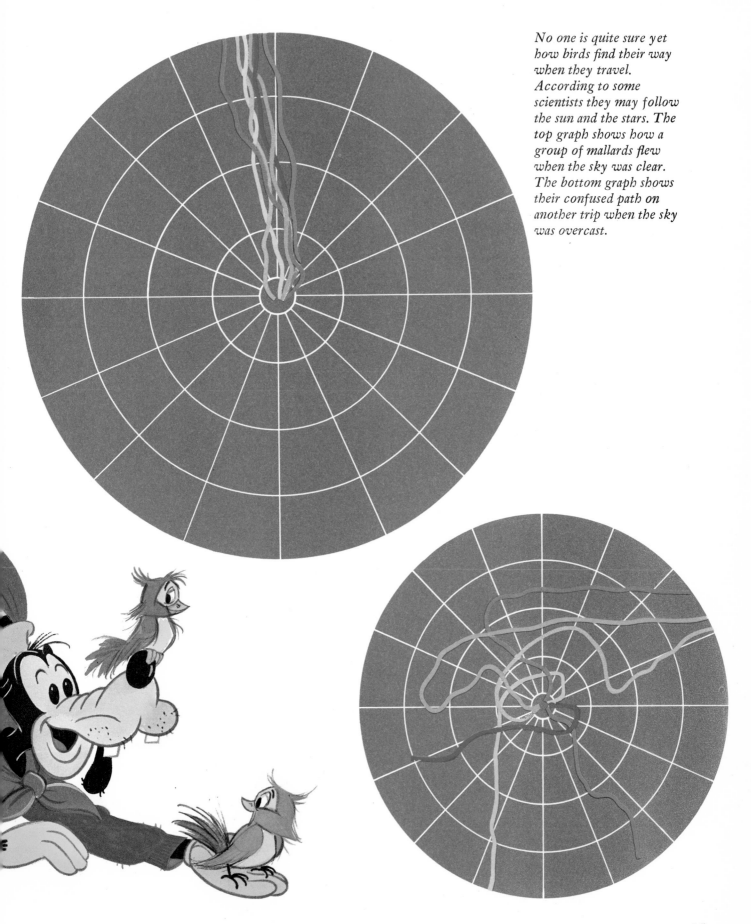

No one is quite sure yet how birds find their way when they travel. According to some scientists they may follow the sun and the stars. The top graph shows how a group of mallards flew when the sky was clear. The bottom graph shows their confused path on another trip when the sky was overcast.

46

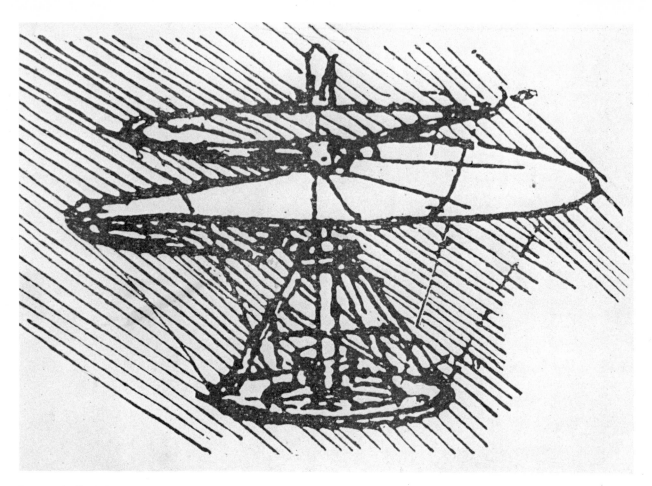

Leonardo Da Vinci was an outstanding painter, sculptor, and architect. He also designed bridges, highways, weapons, and flying machines. One of his most ambitious efforts was a helicopter, a sketch of which is seen above. Da Vinci was never able to construct the machine from his sketches because materials to build flying machines were not available in the 1500's.

FLYING LIKE A BIRD

To poor old stuck-on-the-ground Goofy, the most marvelous thing about birds is that they can fly. It makes me downright jealous to watch them swooping and soaring overhead. Scientists tell me birds can fly because their bodies are well adapted to the job. They have light, strong skeletons and some of their bones are specially shaped for flying. The feathers that cover their bodies and wings form a perfect, flexible surface for flight. No wonder that earthbound men first tried to fly by imitating birds and strapping feathery contraptions on their bodies.

The great 15th-century Italian artist and scientist Leonardo da Vinci filled notebooks with detailed drawings of birds in flight. Using these drawings as a basis, he designed elaborate devices for lifting men into the air. One of the devices even had a crank that made the wings flap up and down. Da Vinci's designs were never tested during his lifetime but one of his designs for a helicopter was built later and flown successfully.

Hundreds of years and thousands of experiments later men succeeded in getting up into the air with the birds. In fact, just as Da Vinci guessed, a modern airplane is designed a lot like a bird.

But even birds must come to earth to eat and rest. In "A Bird Came Down the Walk," a glimpse of their life on land

47

was captured by the American poetess, Emily Dickinson.

A bird came down the walk:
He did not know I saw;
He bit an angleworm in halves
And ate the fellow raw.

And then he drank a dew
From a convenient grass,
And then hopped sidewise to the wall
To let a beetle pass.

I have talked quite a bit about dogs and birds by now and I hope my other animal friends didn't mind not being chosen first. If they were hurt, I apologize, particularly to all my friends in the cat kingdom who may be wondering why they have not heard a single meow so far. Well, dear cats and dear readers, your old friend Goofy is going to take up the subject of cats immediately, before anyone can complain about them being left out of my book.

The pigeons of St. Mark's Square in Venice, Italy, are as familiar a part of the scenery as its great buildings. It has been the law since the 12th century that the citizens of Venice feed all the pigeons that live there.

49

CAT LOVERS AND CAT HATERS

To a cat lover the precious four-footed animal is a bundle of fur covering a very intelligent being. To the cat hater this same animal is a source of terror. For as long as men have lived on earth the world has been divided into these two groups.

The ancient Egyptians were the first group we know of that worshiped cats. It is possible that because they were a farming people, the Egyptians came to appreciate the virtues of cats. For one thing, cats helped to protect the crops by destroying field mice. No matter what the exact reason, cats came to be sacred animals in Egypt. They were worshiped in temples, loved and protected while they lived, embalmed and wrapped in mummy bandages when they died. There were even cat cemeteries in the city of Bubastis and other places in Egypt. Egyptian statues of cats are among the most beautiful that have ever been made.

Throughout history there have been other individuals and nations that cared

Staring at us is a black domestic cat. He is beautiful, but there are many who say that if a black cat crosses your path you will have bad luck. Don't believe a word of it!

deeply about cats. It is said the prophet Mohammed—the founder of the Muslim religion—had a cat that he loved very dearly. One day when Mohammed was deep in prayer his cat lay peacefully on his arm. Soon the cat was purring contentedly and had fallen asleep. When Mohammed at last completed his prayers he decided that he could not disturb his dear pet. He carefully cut off the sleeve of his robe so that the sleeping cat would not have to be awakened. The followers of Mohammed later established a cat hospital in the city of Damascus and made it the law that a cat could not be killed or harmed.

Many famous writers and artists are well-known for their love of cats. Among them was the 18th-century English writer Dr. Samuel Johnson whose pet cat enjoyed a diet of oysters. Another cat fancier was the American writer Mark Twain who said, "A home without a cat; and a well-fed, well-petted, and properly revered cat, may be a perfect home, perhaps, but how can it prove its title?"

The other side of the cat story is told by the ailurophobes—the fancy word for cat haters. Shakespeare mentioned cats often in his plays—but always with a shiver of dislike, or so it seems. The 19th-century French Emperor Napoleon I had

51

Two of these cats are quiet and domestic. One, however, is quite wild. Above: a bob cat. Opposite, top: a domestic calico cat. Opposite, bottom: a seal-point Siamese cat.

little trouble expanding his empire to include most of Western Europe. But he is said to have broken out in a cold sweat if a cat came near him.

Even some of the best-known poems about cats tell the same two-sided story. It was surely not a cat lover who wrote:

There was a young lady of Niger
Who smiled as she road on a Tiger:
They came back from the ride
With the lady inside
And the smile on the face of the Tiger.

Speaking of these big cats, the tigers, it is only fair to remember one of the most famous poems ever written about these giants. It is called "Tiger! Tiger!" and was written by the 18th-century English poet, William Blake. It begins:

Tiger! Tiger! burning bright
In the forests of the night
What immortal hand or eye
Could frame thy fearful symmetry?

Maybe it is just this mixture of strength, terror, and beauty that makes the cat lovers what they are and turns otherwise strong men into cat haters.

Because cats are so popular people have spent a lot of time watching them and trying to draw conclusions from their behavior. Black cats, it is said, should never be allowed to cross your path, but no one can explain why. In some parts of the United States it is believed that if a cat washes her face it is a sign that the weather will be fair. All that we know for sure is that cats spend a lot of time cleaning themselves! We also know for a fact that it is only a superstition that cats have nine lives. They are skillful hunters and climbers who have survived only by being as careful as you or I have to be as

we go about our daily business. All these cat tales remind me of other little stories about man's best friends, and I'd like to tell them to you.

SOME "WHYS" ABOUT MAN'S BEST FRIENDS

I have some answers scattered around to some questions you might have had about some of man's best friends. Here goes!

Why do cranes sleep on only one foot?

Because if they lifted up the other one, too, they'd fall down. O.K., I was only kidding. Actually cranes have become a symbol of guardianship or watchfulness because before falling asleep—on only

Members of the ape family, baboons live in large troops on the ground, among rocks or in forests. They are found mostly in the wilds of Asia and Africa.

one foot—they look around to be sure that there is no danger nearby. If they have the slightest suspicion of trouble they grab a stone in one claw and stand ready to throw it. This way they stay awake and as soon as they start dozing off the claw relaxes, the stone drops, and the watchman wakes up again!

Why is it wrong to call the lion "the king of the forest" or "the king of the jungle?"

Because lions don't live in the jungle. They live on open land where there are plenty of shrubs, bushes, and high grass.

Why can dogs be called with "silent" whistles?

Because dogs can hear sounds that are pitched higher than human ears can hear, and that's the sound the high-pitched whistle makes.

Why do cats always land on their feet?

Because when a cat falls it instinctively uses its tail for balance and changes its body's center of gravity so that its paws are always pointed toward the ground.

Why are dachshunds called dachshunds?

In German *dachs* means "badger" and *hund* means "hound." In the old days these dogs where famous badger hunters and the name has stuck with them, even when they are city-dwellers.

Why do cat's eyes shine at night?

The green glare of a cat's eyes at night is called eyeshine. It comes from a lining at the back of the cat's eyes, which makes the cat see better in the dark and causes the glow one sees in their eyes.

Why are canaries called canaries?

These lovely yellow song birds were first found on the Canary Islands off the west coast of Africa in the 16th century by European sailors who were enchanted by their singing. Some of the birds were taken back to Europe and soon became the treasured and pampered pets of noblemen.

And speaking of the sailors of long ago, I see it is time to start on a new adventure. Let's set sail on the world's water highways.

Right: There are many kinds of canaries, but the wild canary is one of the loveliest. Opposite page: A lioness stalks through grasslands searching for food.

ADVENTURERS OF THE SEVEN SEAS

"Water is excellent," wrote the famous Greek poet Pindar, and I'm sure you'd all agree. "Water covers about 70 percent of the earth's surface," say the scientists, and I'm sure you all knew that already. The largest bodies of water are called seas and oceans.

These seas and oceans have presented a tremendous challenge to men since the first caveman edged away from the campfire to start exploring the world around him. In ancient times men traveled cautiously from one familiar coast to another. It is said that the Greeks first sailed the seas surrounding their land by carefully moving from one island to another nearby island. But as ships and the knowledge of navigation improved, men pushed out far beyond their familiar landscapes to discover unknown lands and seas.

If you were to ask me which period in the history of seafaring I found to be the most exciting, I would have to think for only a second. My answer would be that

The seven seas, like the continents, have been the source of myths and legends that have fascinated mankind since the earliest times. The vast seas and oceans were another unknown world to conquer.

it was the age of the great sailing ships. Or, to be more exact, the period of the great European voyages of discovery and exploration of distant, unknown lands and uncharted seas.

The most famous of all these, of course, was Christopher Columbus' voyage because with only two caravels. . . .

"No," you object, "there were three!"

Hold on a minute. Give old Goofy a chance to finish his sentence! Let me explain this tricky point. You see Columbus set out to discover what he believed were the Indies with *two* caravels and *one* larger ship—the flagship *Santa María.* You see, the important feature of the old sailing ship was the presence of at least three masts. The *Santa María* had three, but the caravels had only two. Now that we have settled that complicated point, I would like to remind you that besides being used for noble purposes like exploration, ships were also used for war and for piracy. In sailing, as in everything else, there was a good side and a bad side. You say you'd like to stick with this topic of pirates for a minute or two? O.K. But let's start out by recalling that there were two kinds of adventurers on the high seas—pirates and privateers.

GOOD MEN AND BAD MEN WHO SAILED THE SEVEN SEAS

Now to explain the fine line of difference between a pirate and a privateer. A pirate was a wicked adventurer, a thief of the sea who raided and looted ships for his own gain. A privateer was considered a brave man of the sea who, with a swift ship and a trusty crew, fought for his own country and often flew his country's flag. Since the ship belonged to the privateer, he had the right to keep all the booty he won for himself. The golden age for these privateers was the 16th century, especially in England under the rule of Queen Elizabeth I. This clever queen knew how to make good use of her privateers and some of them, such as John Hawkins, Sir Francis Drake, and Sir Walter Raleigh, became famous and wealthy and were considered great patriots.

But let's keep our conversation in proper historical order by first talking

One of the first great naval battles of modern times was fought near Lepanto (now Naupaktos), Greece. In the battle the combined forces of Spain, Venice, and the Papal States defeated the Turks, who were trying to win control of the Mediterranean Sea.

about pirates, since they were around a long time before the privateers came on the scene.

The truth of the matter is that pirates had been sailing the seven seas as long as there had been ships to rob. The earliest stories of piracy come from the Mediterranean Sea where trading by ships began centuries and centuries ago. According to ancient historians the great Roman leader Julius Caesar was himself the victim of a pirate's attack. He was returning from a visit to Asia Minor when the ship was boarded by pirates and he was taken captive. Caesar sent a message to his family asking that they supply the ransom that the pirates demanded as the price for his release. In due time the ransom money came, Caesar was set free, and the pirates began to celebrate. Their cele-

Two of the most famous English privateers were Sir Walter Raleigh (left), who helped colonize America, and Sir Francis Drake (right), who helped defeat Spain's "Invincible Armada."

bration ended suddenly, however, when their party was surrounded by a group of Caesar's men who captured all the pirates easily.

Among the most famous of the sea robbers of the olden days were the Vikings, who sailed out of northern Europe in their longboats between about A.D. 700 and 1000. These roving bands of daring seamen were less interested in attacking other ships than in robbing cities and towns along the coast of Europe and on its inland waterways. At the peak of their power they pushed far south into Russia and Turkey and occupied parts of Ireland, England, France, Italy, and Spain.

But the pirates who really put piracy on the map were the men who roamed the seas during the settlement of the Americas. After the Spanish had conquered and colonized parts of Central and South America and the islands of the West Indies, rumors of great wealth in the New World began to spread. Spain was growing rich on the treasures of the Americas—gold, silver, and precious gems. Other countries grew envious of the Spaniards' new-found wealth and attacks on Spanish ships headed homeward from the Americas became common. Men from Spain's greatest rival of that time—England—added a new flavor to piracy. Sir Francis Drake and Sir Walter Raleigh

actually helped England to gain command of the seas over Spain by committing what were really acts of piracy.

Drake was on a trading voyage to the West Indies when the ship he commanded and the small fleet sailing with it were attacked by Spaniards. Only Drake's ship and one other vessel escaped from the fight. Drake vowed to get his revenge on the Spaniards.

Drake's ambition fitted in well with Queen Elizabeth's ambition to make England the greatest of all naval powers. With his Queen's consent and support Drake raided some of Spain's colonies in the America's. He also attacked Spanish ships, not only to annoy them, but to rob them as well.

In 1572 Drake led a daring attack on a town in Panama, with only a handful of men. They succeeded in capturing several tons of silver that were to go to the king of Spain.

Five years later the Queen gave Drake permission to lead the first English ex-

Among the weapons carried by the Spanish conquerors of the Americas were these swords made in Toledo, Spain. Toledo blades are still famous today. The excellent quality of the swords comes from expert craftsmanship. Top: A workman welds a part of the sword. Middle: A pattern is etched on a blade. Bottom: A test for flexibility.

pedition to the Pacific Ocean. In his ship the *Golden Hind*, Drake crossed the treacherous Straits of Magellan at the tip of South America. He then passed through what is now called Drake Passage. Drake then sailed north and attacked Spanish settlements along the east coast of South America. Now, with a full cargo of gold and silver, Drake set out in search of the Northwest Passage across the North American continent. He failed to find the waterway and was forced to start for home by way of the long route across the Pacific. Drake was the first Englishman to make the trip across the Pacific. He was also the first European to follow in the footsteps of the great navigator Ferdinand Magellan. But unlike Magellan, Drake lived to tell the tales of his adventures on the high seas.

In 1580, when Drake returned to England after his three-year voyage, he was knighted by the Queen. The Spaniards, however, were growing angry at the way things were going for them. They

Pirates and privateers did not capture all the treasure of Spain's New World colonies. According to legend, a part of the treasure is hidden under one of the shells in this richly ornamented House of Shells in Salamanca, a city in Spain.

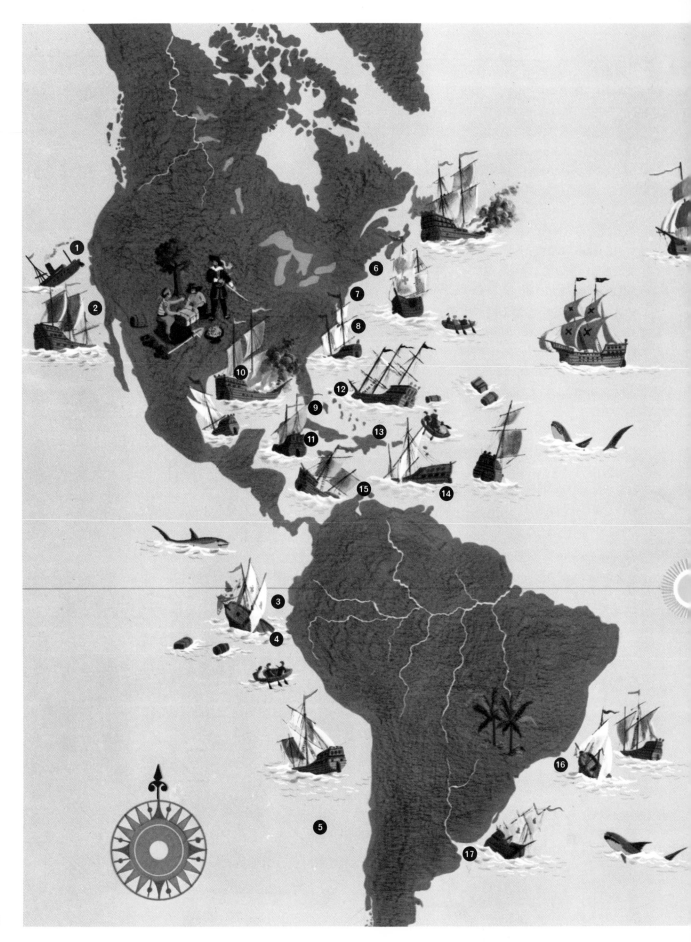

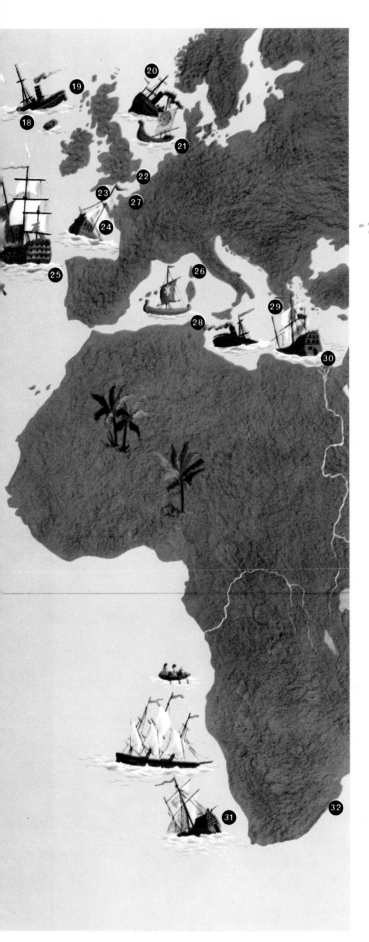

Rich treasures lie buried beneath the sea. This map shows where some ships laden with treasure went down and where some treasure is said to be buried. 1) Rio de Janeiro off San Francisco. 2) San Sebastian off California, 1754. 3) Santa Cruz, 1680, 4) Todos Santos, 1799, and 5) Santa Cecilia, 1702, all off the west coast of South America. 6) The Republic, 1909, 7) Ussard, 1790, and 8) Merida, all off the east coast of the United States. 9) Twenty-eight galleons, sixteen caravels, the Gasparilla, and the Santa Rosa, all off the tip of Florida. 10) Treasure buried by pirates on the Gulf Coast of Texas, 1700. 11) Eleven galleons sunk in Matanzas Bay. 12) Fifteen galleons in the Bahamas. 13) Santisima Concepcion, Tortuga Bay, 1775. 14) San Fernando off St. Lucia, 1597. 15) Five galleons off La Ceiba. 16) Thirty-two galleons, and 17) the Aurora, 1772, all off east coast of South America. 18) Empress of Britain, 1940. 19) The Mull Island, 1588. 20) The Hampshire, 1917. 21) The General Barker, 1781, and Lutine, 1798. 22) Pereira, 1588. 23) Anson, 1891. 24) Off Brest, France: The Drummond Castle, 1896, the Elisabethville, 1917, and the Egypt, 1922. 25) Sixteen galleons, Vigo Bay. 26) "Treasure of Rommel" off Corsica, 1943. 27) Télémaque, 1790. 28) Glenartney, 1918. 29) Bay of Pylos: Guerienne, 1817, and Captain Bey, 1827. 30) Six of Napoleon's ships, off Egypt, 1798. 31) Forty-two frigates, 1716, and 32) Grosvenor, 1782, off South Africa.

69

planned an invasion of England and started to build a great fleet. But Drake sailed into the harbor of Cadiz, Spain, with his own small fleet of ships and set fire to many of the Spanish ships that were under construction there. He even boasted that he had singed the king of Spain's beard! Unwilling to accept defeat, the Spaniards sent an Armada of about 130 ships into the English Channel in 1588. Drake was the vice-admiral of the fleet that destroyed many of the ships of the Armada. England was finally assured of her supremacy on the seas.

THE REAL PIRATES

Not all of the pirates—or privateers—can be thought of as heroes like Drake. Some were the cruelest and most bloodthirsty men who have ever lived. Their lives were dedicated to robbery. The lives of other people meant little to them, and they killed anyone who interfered with their thievery. The main hide-outs of these wicked pirates were in the islands of the Caribbean Sea and in the better hidden harbors of the Spanish Main (South

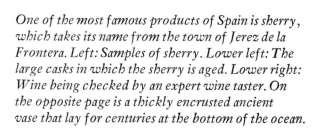

One of the most famous products of Spain is sherry, which takes its name from the town of Jerez de la Frontera. Left: Samples of sherry. Lower left: The large casks in which the sherry is aged. Lower right: Wine being checked by an expert wine taster. On the opposite page is a thickly encrusted ancient vase that lay for centuries at the bottom of the ocean.

America) and the American Main (eastern North America).

One of these men, Sir Henry Morgan, was widely known and feared. In 1671, during his most famous adventure, he stormed Panama City and robbed its storehouses of gold and precious jewels. Yet even this wicked man captured the imagination of the people of his time, and he was knighted by the English King, Charles II. Later he was made lieutenant governor of the English colony of Jamaica in the Caribbean. Surprisingly he tried to banish pirates from the seas. Before he died in 1688, he believed that the last sea robber had been frightened off

forever. How wrong he was soon became clear.

Soon ships were seen flying the terrifying black flag of the pirates—the Jolly Roger with its skull and crossbones. The most famous of the new crew of outlaws was the man called Blackbeard. His long beard was braided and tied with ribbons.

In 1930 and 1931 two pleasure ships built by the Roman Emperor Caligula were raised from the bottom of Lake Nemi in Central Italy. These fantastic vessels were said to be floating cities with hanging gardens and palaces. The picture on this page is of a similar but imaginary floating city with the long, long name Tessarakonteres. *It was supposedly built by the Egyptian Pharaoh Ptolemy IV.*

73

Over one shoulder he carried a sling filled with pistols, while a cutlass glistened on his other side. This ruthless man met his match in a hand-to-hand fight with an officer of the British Navy in 1718.

Along with legends of terror and of buried treasure, men like Blackbeard, William Kidd, and Bartholomew Roberts (the gentleman pirate who forbade his men to drink, swear, or gamble) left a code of rules. As terrible as the pirates were to their enemies, they were nearly always loyal to each other. It was a rule that they cared for each other if they became sick or wounded. On nearly all pirate ships strict laws of democracy were practiced. Captains were elected by a majority vote and even the way booty was to be divided was decided on before hand and written down.

The freedom of the pirates to roam and rob on the seven seas ended in the 19th century. At this time the major nations of the world built up navies so strong that no single pirate ship could match them. One by one the last hide-outs in the Caribbean, the Mediterranean, and elsewhere disappeared. Nowadays the closest we are likely to come to a pirate is at the movies or in an exciting adventure story, like Robert Louis Stevenson's *Treasure Island*.

A view of the harbor at Tortuga (Turtle) Island off northern Haiti in the Caribbean Sea is shown on the opposite page. It was a favorite pirate hideaway because of its excellent harbors. Left: An iron ring for securing a pirate ship in a secluded harbor. Below, right: The pirate crews often had to hide in the dense undergrowth or deeply hidden caves of the islands. Below, left: "The Street of Gold" was the name given to the stony path along which gold was smuggled out of South America to waiting pirate ships in Panama and other Central American countries. It is obvious that a pirate's life was rarely safe.

RICHES FROM FAR AWAY LANDS

All this talk about adventurers sailing the seas has given me an appetite for ocean travel. It also reminds me that some men traveled to the ends of the earth for reasons other than waging war or robbing ships.

As you know, one of man's most common traits in his curiosity. I'm talking about worthwhile curiosity, not the idle kind that turns him into a busybody.

It was this good kind of curiosity that led men to wonder just who, or what, lived over the crest of the hill, beyond the mountains, and over the seas. To put it simply, curiosity was the beginning of exploration—the great human adventure which, with interplanetary flights, has placed man on the path to knowledge of the universe in which he lives.

Sometimes curiosity was more than just a desire to learn something new. Man's curiosity led him to seek new riches in distant and unknown lands.

In the middle of the 6th century, for instance, the Emperor Justinian sent two

During the early 17th century, adventurers in search of lands where tea plants were plentiful came upon the natural green riches of the island of Ceylon. Many tea plantations were soon established.

monks from Constantinople to the Far East. Their job was to get hold of the "seeds" of that "mysterious plant that produces silk." The monks did their job carefully. They smuggled the cocoons out of China, because it was against the law to export them. The secret of making silk thus was brought to the West.

Another secret of the East came to Europe more by accident than by plan, and what a yummy secret it was. In A.D. 1187, during one of the Crusades to free the Holy Land, the Muslim Sultan Saladin entertained some of the Christian nobles he had captured by feeding them rose water iced with the snows of a nearby mountain. This may have been the beginning of the lovely ice cream and sherbert era, which has made life so much more delicious for all of us.

Still another traveler who probably tasted the delicious flavored ices of the East was Marco Polo. He made a long journey across Asia into lands completely unknown to the Europeans of his time—the 13th century. His traveling companions were his father and his uncle. The Polos were jewel traders. On the trip that Marco took with his father and uncle, however, they also acted as the Pope's

Once a silkworm has completed the process of eating mulberry leaves and has grown to a certain size, it begins to spin its cocoon in a continuous thread around its body.

A cluster of silkworm cocoons. After the silkworm has spun its thread for about 10 days, the cocoon is heated to destroy the silkworm. The cocoon is washed in warm water to free the threads.

ambassadors to the great Kublai Khan, the ruler of much of the East. Marco Polo's description of his travels in the East electrified the people of Europe. One of the Chinese products he brought back to Europe had a great effect on the cooking of Italy and eventually of the whole world. Can you guess what it was? Spaghetti, of course—a food that is now almost as popular as ice cream.

FOODS THAT TRAVELED

Man's discovery of different foods has really been going on since the earliest times. Wheat, which was probably first grown in Egypt and the Indus Valley, gradually spread into Europe. By 2500 B.C. the first wheat was being grown in distant Denmark.

Other foods that began to travel early in history were olives, sugar, and rice. Greek sailors carrying olives from their country introduced this delicate food to distant lands. And Greek soldiers who accompanied Alexander the Great on his campaign in India in the 4th century B.C. brought back the "sweet stick of the east"—sugarcane. Rice was probably first grown in India and then carried by traders to Asian countries, such as Japan and China, where it has become a staple of the diet.

THE SEARCH FOR SPICES

One of the oldest ways known to man of keeping foods fresh was to salt them. As a result salt became a highly prized commodity. Roman soldiers cheerfully accepted part of their pay in salt, and to this day we speak of receiving a salary, a word that comes from the Latin *salarium*, which means "salt money."

Europeans gradually learned about other spices and seasonings from travelers to other lands. In a time when there was hardly any way to keep food fresh for long, spices were most important for use as preservatives and to disguise the taste of meat and vegetables that were not as fresh as they should have been. Rare spices such as pepper, ginger, and cinnamon also came into use as money because they were so scarce and precious.

The search for shorter routes to the sources of these rare spices, as well as the search for gold and silver for coins that would make trade simpler, led to some of the greatest of man's explorations. Clearly the nations that mastered the shortest route to the Orient would soon be the masters of Europe . . . and of much of the world. The race was on, with the sailors of Portugal and Spain in the lead.

A magnificent Viking wagon that was found in Denmark recalls the Viking sailors who may have introduced salted codfish and other dishes to southern Europe.

Now, as you well know, Columbus never did find the shorter route to the East Indies and their wealth of spices. He did discover something that proved more important—the New World. It proved to be an enormous treasure chest.

One of the new spices Columbus discovered in America was allspice. He also introduced Europe to such vegetables as lima beans, corn, and the source of chocolate—the cacao bean. Other foods that returned to the Old World with later explorers included potatoes, tomatoes, pineapples, bananas, and avocados. The exchange was complete because Columbus introduced sugarcane to the New World, and later explorers brought with them such European vegetables as spinach, asparagus, cauliflower, and garlic.

A romantic painting of Christopher Columbus's landing in the New World on the morning of October 12, 1492. Columbus had set out on his great voyage to find a new, shorter route to the fabled Spice Islands of the Indies. He thought he had found them but, of course, he had discovered the Americas.

Potatoes soon became an important part of the European diet, but tomatoes had a harder time finding their way to the table, or even into the kitchen! In both Italy and France people thought the tomato was simply a flower to be carefully tended in the garden for its lovely blossom. In France it was called a *pomme d'amour*, or "love apple," and it was so highly prized that gallant gentlemen gave it to their ladies as a token of love.

SOME LIKE IT HOT

Today people drink billions of gallons of tea and coffee prepared in hundreds of different ways. But these beverages were not always popular. Actually, it took a long time for these drinks to spread from their countries of origin and gain world-wide popularity.

There is an ancient Chinese legend that tells of the Chinese Emperor Shen-Nung who was sitting in his garden one fine day in the year 2737 B.C. A few wild tea leaves drifted off a nearby bush into his pot of drinking water and the art of tea-drinking was born. Word of this new beverage spread very slowly. It was not until the mid-16th century that a book was published in Italy describing the habit of tea-drinking among the Chinese. And it was almost 50 years later before the first tea was imported into Europe by the Dutch, who have the honor of being Europe's first tea-drinkers.

The popularity of this newly dis-covered drink grew slowly because it was so expensive. But in spite of the cost, the idea of having a refreshing cup of tea caught on. Tea-drinking added its special flavor to life and to the language. The little boxes in which tea was packed by the Chinese weighed a *kati* or *catty* from which we get our word for a small box, "caddy." The drink itself gets its name from the word *t'e*, which was used by some Chinese.

Before long the British founded the East India Company to trade with the nations of the Orient, and the price of tea began to go down. The drink was no longer saved for a small after-dinner cup. It became a beverage to be used almost anytime one felt a bit hungry and sleepy. We're told that a French lady named Madame de Sevigne first added milk to tea. Soon she had all her friends doing the same thing. Another influential lady was the Duchess of Bedford who lived in England in the early 19th century. It was she—some say—who invented the tea party by having a cup of tea and a slice of cake at four or five o'clock in the afternoon. Soon she had her friends join her and a new meal was added to the daily eating schedule.

An interesting addition to the art of tea-drinking was made by the Russians. Their tea is made in a samovar—a large urn that holds about 40 cups of water heated by a small flame from a gas or charcoal heater. At the top of the urn is a teapot in which the strong essence of tea is kept. This strong brew is poured into a glass until it is about one-quarter full and then diluted with water from the samovar. It was the Russians, too, who thought of adding something sweeter than sugar to their tea. Some use a spoonful of jam!

A 17th-century navigational map that shows how much men had learned of the New World in the 3 centuries after Columbus made his discovery of the area. By this time in history much of the region was already well-known to European explorers and colonists who had also learned how to eat such "Indian" foods as turkey, potatoes, and corn.

83

Above: One of the many sidewalk cafés in Paris. They offer visitors a place to relax and chat and have some refreshments. Opposite page: Bananas grown on a plantation in Costa Rica, Central America, are loaded on a conveyer system. The bananas are later packed and sent to a nearby port from which they will be shipped throughout the world.

The only thing that is known with certainty about coffee's start on the road to fame is that it was probably first grown in Kaffa, Ethiopia. And Kaffa is, of course, the root for our word "coffee."

It is believed that by the 6th century the Persians had learned that chewing coffee beans kept one awake. They were probably the ones who took coffee seeds to the Arabian Peninsula. The Arabs took a giant step forward by cooking the bitter seeds in water. This made a strong, tasty brew, which, with a little sugar added, became popular in all the Muslim lands.

It took until the 17th century for coffee to make its way into Europe. The people of Vienna, Austria, like to claim the honor of opening the first coffeehouse in the year 1684. According to their version of the story, when the Turkish Army fled from its defeat after the second siege of Vienna, it left bags of coffee behind. The thrifty Viennese experimented with these beans, made coffee, added a dish of pastries, and invented the coffeehouse. It makes a nice story, although it is not quite true. Records show that the first coffeehouse was probably opened in Constantinople in 1540. The city of Oxford in England had its first coffeehouse in 1650. These *cafés*, as they are still often called (after the French word for coffee), became the center of a whole new way of life. Newspapers were provided free to customers, and the intellectuals of the city or town would gather there to argue about the important issues of the day while they sipped coffee and nibbled on delicious pastries.

Naturally all this opportunity for sitting around and talking worried some governments. They were suspicious that plots against them might be brewing along with the coffee. King Charles II of England was so frightened by these places that he ordered them shut down. This move did not help his popularity at all. He was forced to reopen the coffeehouses whether or not he liked what was happening there.

Well, my friends, I guess we have thought enough for a while about good food and rare drinks. But, before we go on to look at another topic, (don't peek!), let's just take a quick look at the globe and think about how faraway some of our foods are grown. There are coconuts from the Philippines, dates from Iraq, cacao beans from Ghana, bananas from Central America, and figs from Greece. Tiny sesame seeds come from El Salvador, and giant containers of olive oil come from Italy. My favorite pistachio nuts come from Iran, and delicious cashews come from India. But now we must stop this talk or we will be too full to move another step!

MAN AND MACHINES

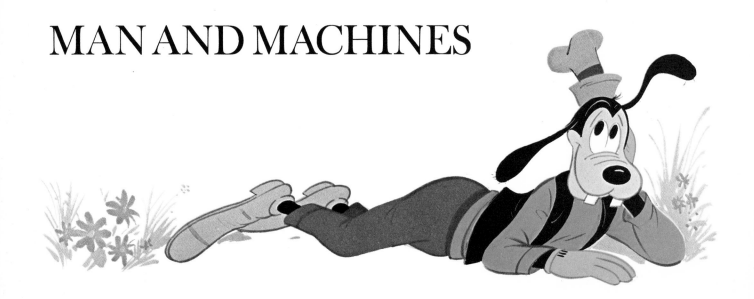

Did you know that there is a species of South American hummingbird whose wings beat at a rate of about 5,000 strokes per minute, or that a hummingbird can rotate its wings almost 180 degrees? This makes it possible for the tiny, graceful bird to hover in place, fly up, down, and backward. Sounds like a tiny, beautiful helicopter, doesn't it? Well, there is one great difference between the bird and a helicopter that you might have already guessed. The hummingbird uses its own energy while the helicopter gets it push from a machine called a motor.

Do you know that if a man could produce energy, in proportion to his weight, the way a hummingbird does, he could develop nearly 40 horsepower. This is the equivalent of a small car engine. And, as you also may have guessed, man never managed to develop that kind of horsepower. Instead he has had to use his clever brain to develop ways to help him get his work done.

The ancient stone city of Zimbabwe, Rhodesia, in Africa may have been the nearly mythical "land of Punt" from which Egypt got some of its gold. Today it is another silent memorial to the men who built without machines.

Years and years ago when man first started to think about how much power it took to build things, he realized a basic fact. One man's strength was pretty feeble compared to the strength of two men working at the same job. And if two men could do a job more easily than one, it was perfectly clear that for big jobs—such as building the pyramids of Egypt and Mexico, for instance—a crew of thousands of strong men could do the job even better. With the help of such simple and ancient machines as levers and pulleys the work could not only be done more quickly, but a lot of the physical force men provided could be furnished by the machines.

The oldest surviving example of this combination of man and machine resulted in the Great Pyramid of Khufu, or Cheops as the Greeks called him, in Egypt. Built nearly 5,000 years ago, the Great Pyramid covers about 13 acres at its base and rises to a height of 481 feet at its peak. The Great Pyramid contains nearly 2,300,000 blocks of neatly cut stone. Every one of these immense blocks weighed about 2 ½ tons. The huge structure boggles the mind, when one realizes that the men who built it had no animals

Above: The hummingbird is nature's helicopter—a tiny bird that can fly and hover in the air. Opposite page: A view of Hadrian's Wall, which at one time stretched over 70 miles across England.

to help with the hauling of the huge stones and no wheels to put under the stones. They used immense logs as rollers and simple levers to lift and move the stones. The most important hand tool they had was a bronze cutting instrument for shaping and decorating the blocks. In this fantastic building project, as in many others of ancient times, men made up for the lack of machines with man-power—human machines.

Other great surviving examples of works built with the primary help of man-power are the Great Wall of China and Hadrian's Wall in Britain. The Great Wall of China was begun during the 3rd century B.C. and completed in the Ming Dynasty (1368–1644). This 1,500 mile-long wall was built entirely by human hands, although some animals were used to bring materials to the building site. Rising 25 feet above the ground and measuring anywhere from 15 to 30 feet wide at the base, the Great Wall was meant to keep invaders from the Mongolian plain out of China. The wall did

not succeed in doing this. But it remains a monument to man's ability to build gigantic structures with his own strength.

Another large but not always successful military wall was built across northern Britain by the Romans. The Romans wanted to keep the inhabitants of Scotland out of their region. It was called Hadrian's Wall, in honor of the Roman emperor during whose reign it was built. The wall was 73½ miles long, 8 feet wide, 6 feet high and bristled with stone forts about a mile apart. Only a little of

this military wall remains—a small reminder of the estimated 100,000 men who labored for 5 years to build it.

What do you suppose the men whose muscles helped to build some of the marvels of the ancient world would say to the laborsaving inventions that have come along? Would they cheer? Strangely enough, judging from the reaction of other men to the inventions of their time, the cheers would have been mixed with fears. As each new device, each new instrument, each new use for new machines

appeared, there were those who turned up their noses. They warned of the terrible dangers that the machines threatened.

But all the worriers did not stop the march of progress. Some unknown men devised the wheel and a new era in transportation began. Still other unknown men learned to use such products of the earth as coal, iron, copper, and tin. The wind was harnessed to move ships with sails. Water was used to power simple machines. It was slowly becoming plain even to the biggest worriers about new-fangled devices that machines could take over even more of man's work. Dreamers dared to dream of the day when animals

One of the greatest works of ancient man is the Great Pyramid of the Pharaoh Khufu, or Cheops, at Gizeh in Egypt. It was considered one of the Seven Wonders of the World and ranks as the largest pyramid ever built. According to the ancient historian Herodotus it took 20 years to build the pyramid. The work of just hauling the stones was broken into 3-month shifts, using the labor of 100,000 men in each shift.

91

An artist's conception of "The Best Friend of Charleston," the first locomotive constructed in the United States. Built at the West Point Foundry Shops in New York City, the locomotive made its first excursion trip on January 15, 1831.

man had tamed over the centuries could be replaced by machines.

The development of the steam engine in England in the 18th century paved the way for a number of machines that both changed man's life and scared some people out of their wits . . . at first.

EXPERIMENTS WITH STEAM ENGINES

In the early years of the 19th century the most comfortable way to travel was by boat over the surface of a river, lake, or ocean. Roads were poor, rock-filled, bumpy, and often muddy or covered with ice. Horses pulling heavy loads of people and goods tired easily. It was clear that there had to be a better, faster way to get around. Experiments using the ideas of James Watt, who had devised a practical steam engine in England in the 18th century, were put to the test.

In 1804 Richard Trevithick, a coal mine operator in Cornwall, England,

made an important test. He replaced the horse-drawn trams that pulled coal from the mines and delivered it to the nearest ironworks with a steam-powered tram engine. The little engine chugged to its destination about 9 miles away, at the magnificent speed of 5 miles an hour. Mr. Trevithick proudly advertised a later engine, the "Catch me who can . . ." as a "mechanical power subduing animal speed."

92

On August 9, 1831, the "De Witt Clinton," the first steam locomotive to be operated in New York State, was placed in service on the Mohawk and Hudson Railroad between Albany and Schenectady.

The British naturally were not eager to share the knowledge of how to build a steam engine with any of their competitors such as the Americans. A fine of two hundred pounds sterling and a year in prison were threatened for the man who let word out about how the Watt engine was constructed. But the news leaked out anyway. In 1804 a daring man named Oliver Evans was seen chugging along the streets of Philadelphia in his *Oructur Amphibolis* ("amphibious digger"). This was a steam-powered contraption that went easily from the street into the Schuylkill River. This extraordinary machine was really a combination boat and wagon with wheels on its body and a rotating paddle in back—all powered by the remarkable Mr. Watt's steam engine.

Oliver Evans' amphibian looked strange, but it did just what he promised. He was full of faith for the future of

steam-driven carriages or railroads. He announced that they would travel "almost as fast as birds fly, 15 or 20 miles an hour. . . ."

It remained for an Englishman, who had not learned to read until he was past 17 years old, to devise the first practical passenger railroad. In 1825, George Stephenson, an employee of the Stockton and Darlington Railway, drove a train on an 8 mile an hour journey. The train was made up of an engine, a tender with water and coal, six wagons with coal and passengers on top of the coal, a wagon loaded with flour and more passengers, and 22 more wagons. Sparks from the engine frightened and sprayed the passengers, but a new age had arrived. By 1851, a quarter century after this adventurous journey, 6,000 miles of railroad track had been laid in Great Britain

As the years passed, new steam locomotives were designed and manufactured. Before long, people were traveling by rail from the east coast of the United States to the west coast—a distance of approximately 3,000 miles.

94

alone. By the year 1869 railroads linked the Atlantic and Pacific coasts of the United States. Horses were almost—but not totally—out of the transportation business. The age of the Iron Horse had dawned. But before it had time to spread to every continent, experiments were begun with an even more remarkable device—the horseless carriage.

THE HORSELESS CARRIAGE

Some historians say that those amazing men, Watt, Trevethick, and Evans, can also claim to be the fathers of the automobile. It is true they showed that a carriage could be pulled by mechanical power. However, it was another kind of engine—the internal combustion engine —that had to be developed before the automobile, owned and driven by millions of people all over the globe, became a reality.

People did experiment with steampowered coaches, but they ran into all kinds of problems. Farmers claimed these coaches frightened their animals. Stagecoach operators naturally disliked the new competition. The owners of toll roads charged extra-high fees because the steam coaches did more damage to the roads than horses' hooves—or so they said! In England the government passed some strange laws to prevent these new self-propelled vehicles from multiplying

Along came the horseless carriage! During the early 1900's automobiles were built in many shapes and sizes. Some of the early models weren't very comfortable. They were built mainly to adapt to the poor roads that existed in the United States at the turn of the century.

too fast. The most famous was the "Red Flag Act" of 1865. This act required that a man walk ahead of each "road locomotive," carrying a red flag warning of the dangerous vehicle that was following him down the road.

Actually there were perfectly sensible reasons to look for a better method than steam to power automobiles. One problem was that chemicals in the water used in automobiles coated the boilers and burners making it necessary to clean them often. Then there was the problem of the car running out of steam at what seemed far too frequent intervals. Finally, people were just plain terrified of what would happen if the steam boiler exploded, although that rarely happened.

Other automobiles were built that were powered by electricity provided by batteries. These cars were smooth running, relatively quiet, had no smelly fumes coming out of the engine, and did not threaten people with dangerous explosions. There was a serious problem with the battery-powered electric cars, however. The batteries had a bad habit of running down as often as every 40 to 60 miles. It was hardly the way to get across country easily.

In 1876 a German inventor named Nikolaus Otto devised an engine operated on coal gas that worked on the four-stroke principle of intake, compression, power, and exhaust. The same principle is operating under the hood of nearly every automobile today, although the fuel used now is gasoline.

Before long automobiles had become the toys of the very rich. Wealthy automobile enthusiasts held races in France, where the roads were best, and up in the Alps, just for the thrill of it. The fashion designers of Paris devised new garments to keep the ladies tidy in the speedy new

The development of new forms of locomotion in the early 19th century gave cartoonists a rich source of inspiration. Above: A French drawing that illustrates a very strange American vehicle shaped like a fish. Opposite page: An English view of the art of locomotion.

Note ... In the Ladies Vehicle the Steam is made with a strong infusion of Gunpowder Tea   **(LOCOMOTION.)**   For an explanation of the Machinery see the next Number of the Edinburg Review.

vehicles. Long scarves, heavy goggles, long coats, and almost elbow length gloves helped keep people relatively clean in those first roofless and wind-shieldless cars.

A sign of the changing times came in 1896 when the Red Flag Act was repealed in England. Autos were here to stay. With each passing year they became easier to operate and safer to drive. Small garages like Henry Ford's in Detroit became the heart of great factories where today autos are manufactured on partly automated assembly lines. What a far cry from the time of the men of Egypt, China, and Rome, when muscles were their only machines.

In this 1829 cartoon an English cartoonist portrayed some of the experiences one might have in a steam-powered, self-propelled vehicle.

THE WORLD OF MAGIC

Well, my friends, it looks as though we are getting to the end of our encyclopedic travels together. If you have been paying attention to all the facts I've gathered for you, you've begun to get the idea that mankind has come a long, long way from the cave days. People have learned a great deal—slowly and sometimes painfully—about their earth, their universe, and themselves. Imagine the first cavemen gathered around the first campfire. Then think of the thousands of years that passed until the first men landed on the moon. It really was "a giant step for mankind" and had been centuries in the making.

In the thousands of years between that first magical campfire and man's landing on the moon, people each day saw things about them that they could not explain. They tried their best to understand, but, being both curious and inventive, they wanted to know why things happened as they did. From these centuries of seeking

Mickey Mouse never told you about his magical powers—or did he? That's something he tries to keep secret. When Mickey is dressed in his special robe and hat, there's no telling what magic he has up his sleeve.

for reasons came some of the superstitions and magical beliefs we still talk about today.

You say you have never knocked on wood, or thrown salt over your shoulder, or been warned not to open an umbrella in the house? Well, maybe you're not superstitious! Except, what do you do on Friday the 13th? Do you worry just a little that things might all go wrong?

Of course you know what I am getting at. Knocking on wood and worrying about Friday the 13th are old superstitions that many people today haven't quite given up—even though they know better! In times gone by, before there were scientific explanations for many occurrences, people could only guess at what made things happen. Imagine how scared our friend the caveman was the first time he saw the sun disappear and the dark night begin. What went through his head when he saw a seed he planted grow into a tall, leafy tree? What was he to do when it rained for days on end, and he couldn't go out hunting or start a fire?

These and a thousand similar problems could not be answered easily. So men invented demons to explain them. If things went well, then the good spirits— 103

To us in the 20th century, the eclipse of the sun is an understandable phenomenon. It does not frighten us nor does it puzzle us. But to the cavemen of prehistoric times the eclipse must have been both awesome and frightening.

This bas-relief of a Roman sacrificial scene hangs in the world-famous Louvre museum in Paris.

to whom a food offering or two was often given—were in charge. If things went wrong, then the bad demons had come into the picture, and steps had to be taken to drive them away and bring back the good demons. Charms (like a four-leaf clover or a rabbit's foot) and counter-magic (such as throwing salt over one's shoulder) were invented to help keep things running well. The good demons had to be kept happy.

All the magical beliefs or superstitions we have today date back to ancient people's attempts to explain the world around them. Now, let's look at some of these superstitions and see how they got started. You may be surprised at the perfectly sensible beginnings of some of these strange beliefs. And don't be surprised that some superstitions still make perfectly good sense today, while science has made others look just plain silly.

THIRTEEN POPULAR SUPERSTITIONS

Let's start with an absolutely ridiculous superstition, the one that has to do with Friday the 13th. In the first place, we have to ask ourselves why people became so uncomfortable about the number 13. It may be, according to some authorities, that when men learned to count, they used their hands or feet. Counting their fingers and their two hands or their two feet, they came up with 12. Anything beyond that was a little strange because it couldn't be seen.

The frightening combination of Friday and 13 may have come from an old Norse legend. According to this tale the goddess Freya was sent away because she was thought to be a witch. Each Friday—a day known as the witches' sabbath—she

105

Above: Witches gather about their caldron as they drop a variety of ingredients into a magic brew. Opposite page: The lovable groundhog acts as a weather forecaster. It is said that if he sees his shadow on February 2 there will be 6 more weeks of winter weather.

met with 11 other witches and, oh my—the devil, too—for a terrible total of 13. It is obvious that worrying about the Friday the 13th makes no sense.

On the other hand let's look at the supersitition that says you should never walk under an open ladder. This is one of the mysterious beliefs that may have started with the strange properties of a triangle (which is the shape of an open ladder). Not walking under a ladder is really good advice, for ladders have been known to collapse, and hammers and buckets of paint have been known to tumble off ladders and hit people. As they say, it is better to be safe than sorry. This, of course, is also the reason for not opening umbrellas in the house. An open umbrella can knock into lamps and ornaments and break them. We could call this bad luck, although clumsiness is more accurate.

It may seem to you that the same kind of anger at clumsiness causes people to be upset when a mirror breaks. After all, a broken mirror can be a nuisance and even dangerous to clean up. A cut from a piece of broken glass is not very nice, expecially when the accident is due to carelessness. But the story of the superstition about broken mirrors is not as simple as that. In ancient times mirrors were extremely rare and precious. To many people, it seemed quite magical that they could see a reflection of themselves in a piece of glass. If the glass broke, they feared that their spirit would be hurt and they would become ill, or die.

It is thought that Stonehenge, a strange ring of giant stones, was built by the people of ancient England as a place of worship. Some scientists

*believe it was used as an astronomical observatory to chart the move-
ments of the stars, moon, and sun.*

A hex sign painted on a barn in Pennsylvania. The Pennsylvania Dutch once considered these hex signs a protection against witchcraft. Opposite: Copy of painting showing Savonarola, the Italian religious reformer, being put to death in 1498. During this period in Europe, superstitions and beliefs in magic, the supernatural, and unseen forces were widespread.

Another magical belief still around also had its origins in an idea about man's health. When you say "God bless you," to someone who has just sneezed, you are being more than polite. This is because long ago people thought that a man's spirit lived in his head as air or breath. If he sneezed he was in danger of driving out this very important spirit. Anyone near the person who sneezed hurried to wish him "God bless you" as counter-magic to keep the spirit from flying away and causing the man to die.

A number of superstitions still with us had their beginnings in ancient man's ideas about nature and animals. For example, if you knock on wood for good luck, it is a reminder of a time when people thought that their gods lived in the trees. A person would touch the bark of the "tree god" if he wanted some special help. He then knocked on the tree to say "thank you" if his wish came true.

Did you ever make a wish by breaking the dried wishbone of a chicken? It is a reminder that people once believed that hens and roosters had special powers and could answer human questions. In the olden days people were also very superstitious about rabbits. They watched the special way in which rabbits ran and they noticed that the bunnies' hind legs touched the ground in front of their forelegs. It was for this reason that the furry

foot of the rabbit's hind leg came to be thought of as a good luck piece—a charm against bad spirits.

Come to think of it, animals have been credited with being in charge of the weather. According to one fine old superstitious rhyme:

Crow on the fence,
Rain will go hence.
Crow on the ground,
Rain will come down.

Everyone knows that if the groundhog comes out of its burrow on February 2nd and sees its shadow, there will be 6 weeks more of winter. The scientists at the weather bureau know how useless that idea is. Test it yourself next February! Unless you'd rather experiment by putting a horsehair in a water trough and waiting (forever) for it to become a snake!

There are loads of superstitions about salt but we have room and time for just a few. Salt has its special place in the world of superstition partly, at least, because it was once so rare. (You remember that I told you a few pages back that salt was once used as money and the Latin word *salarium*—"salt money"—gave us our word "salary.") Salt was also very useful for preserving foods. It does not take much thinking to realize why the ancients gave salt all kinds of special meanings. They thought that by sprinkling salt on a bird's tail they could capture it more easily. The truth of the matter is that any added weight on the bird's tail would have made it easier to catch.

In olden days people thought that if they spilled salt it was a warning from the salt spirits that an evil demon that would cause fights was nearby. To ward off that evil spirit (and a bloody nose) a little more salt was quickly thrown over the left shoulder where the mean spirits were supposed to be hiding.

MAGIC INTO SCIENCE

There was one problem that superstitions could not solve—how to cut down on the amount of work people had to do. The magical solution that came into people's minds was an automatic machine with the brains and skills of a man.

The name "robot" for this creature was invented long after the idea had been hatched. It comes from a 1920 play called *R.U.R.* (*Rossum's Universal Robots*) by the Czech playwright Karel Capek. The Czech word *robota* means "work" or "compulsory service," and that's just what these mechanical men were to do—work!

But, you can believe your friend Goofy, no idea is ever completely original. Even Karel Capek, inventor of the word "robot," was inspired by earlier legends.

Strangely enough, one of the earliest of these legends was set in Capek's own Czechoslovakia—in the capital city of Prague, in fact. Prague is a city of golden church spires, mysterious winding streets, and narrow alleys that seem to have witnessed more history than you could put into 20 encyclopedias.

In one part of the old city of Prague is the old Jewish quarter with its houses, synagogues, and a very ancient cemetery. The most famous grave in that cemetery is that of the High Rabbi Judah Loew, who lived in the 16th century.

Rabbi Loew is said to have made a clay figure that looked like a man. It was called the golem. The golem magically came to life when the *shem*—a strange formula written on parchment—was placed in his

A robot can come in any shape or size and it can even resemble a human being. If it is built properly, the robot can perform a wide variety of mechanical tasks.

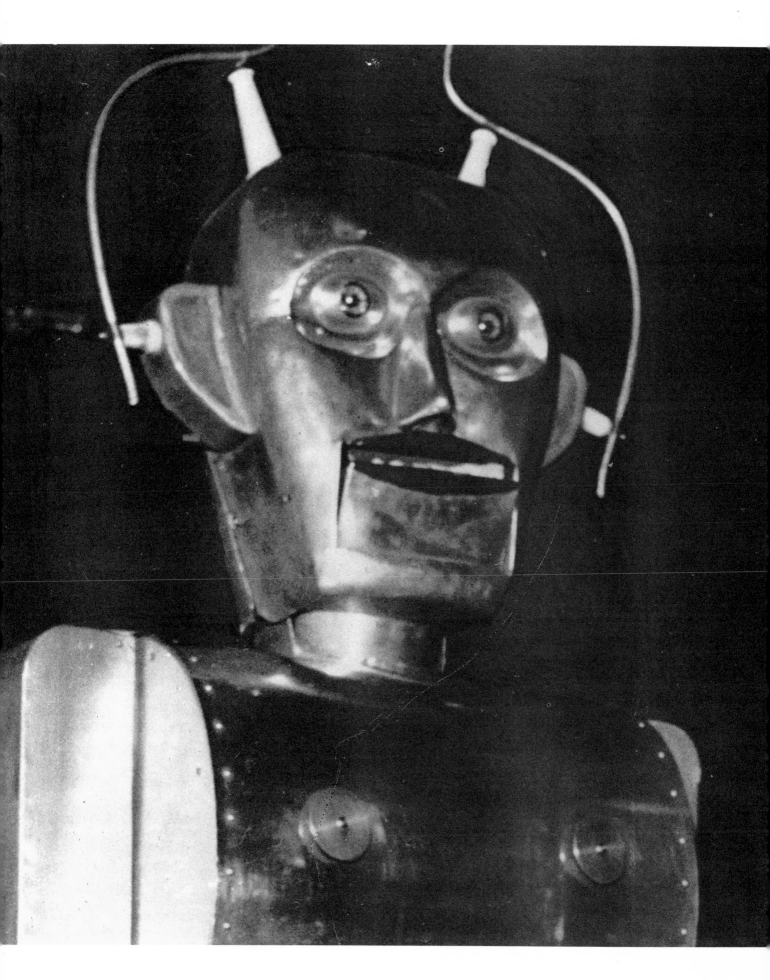

mouth, or, according to some people, laid on his forehead. However it was done, the golem then rose slowly, rubbed his eyes, stretched, and, using the words of the psalm, said to Rabbi Loew, "What do you require of me, master?"

The hundreds of stories and plays that have been written about the golem have given many different answers to the question, "What do you require of me . . . ?" Most people believe that Rabbi Loew simply used the golem as a servant. Because the rabbi was a very kind and religious man, he always remembered to take the *shem* out of the golem's mouth on the eve of the Jewish sabbath, Friday at sunset. It was only proper that the golem should have his day of rest when the rabbi did.

Then there came a Friday when the rabbi must have been very busy thinking about other things. He forgot to take the *shem* out of the golem's mouth. Disaster struck! The golem ran around the old Jewish quarter of the town like a crazy man, uprooting trees, terrifying children, and generally making a tremendous amount of trouble. The Rabbi heard all this and rushed out into the street to chase his golem. He finally caught up with him in front of the synagogue and quickly removed the *shem* from his mouth (or forehead). The golem fell to the ground in a thousand pieces. And, so the legend says, these thousand pieces were reverently picked up and placed in the attic of the synagogue, where they still may be seen by those who are brave enough to go into that dark and mysterious place.

Prague, the capital city of Czechoslovakia, dates from the 9th century. It lies on the banks of the Vltava River. It is a city filled with history and legends. Opposite page: The ancient cemetery in the old Jewish quarter of Prague.

Because the rabbi was supposed to have such great powers people still visit his grave in hopes of getting some help from him . . . or his robot. Visitors to the tomb often can be seen slipping a bit of paper under a stone. These modern *shems* seem to increase dramatically during examination time at Prague's schools and universities! But no one is certain about whether this method of studying helps or not.

MONSTERS AND MACHINES

The idea of a robot to do the work of man seems to have had a special appeal for writers. Rabbi Loew's golem was recreated in a legend that tells of a meeting between the French King Louis XI and a great magician named Frollo who devised a robot. The robot was a pitiful figure who

fell in love with a beautiful girl. This may have provided the inspiration for the famous 19th century novel *The Hunchback of Notre Dame*, written by Victor Hugo. This sad story, which is set in Paris long, long ago, tells of the love of the hunchback Quasimodo for the beautiful Esmeralda.

The most famous of all the robots in literature was created by Mary Shelley, the wife of the famous English poet Percy Bysshe Shelley. During a depressing, rainy summer in Switzerland, the Shelleys read each other ghost stories and then started to invent new ones. From this simple start came *Frankenstein*. In Mary Shelley's version of this story, Frankenstein is a Swiss student of philosophy who has learned how to give life to nonliving things. He collected human bones and made a human figure of them, which he brought to life. Like poor Quasimodo, Frankenstein's oversize creation was so hideous that people were terrified by the sight of him. Naturally the poor creature was nearly mad with sorrow at the way people treated him. Gradually he grew insane and went on a rampage of killing. By now even his creator, Frankenstein, was horrified by the monster he had made and chased him across the world. Finally Frankenstein found his monster in the Arctic and was murdered by him. The monster then disappeared, only to be reborn in countless movies about his frightening adventures.

It is no wonder, considering how some of these fictional robots behaved, that some people are still a little frightened when they hear the word robot or think about any automatic machine that does its work at the touch of a finger on a button. Actually, to get the proper view of things, you should only think of how nice it is to get water from a fountain by turning a handle or how happy you are when a bar of candy falls into your hand from a vending machine.

Speaking of these machines and others like them reminds me, your always encyclopedic Goofy, that such machines are not as modern as you might think.

A 13th-century traveler to the Great Khan of the Mongols tells of a really marvelous machine he saw there. It was a large silver fountain shaped like a tree. Three gold snakes with emerald eyes were twisted around the tree's base.

When important company arrived at the court of the Khan, an angel made of gold and silver sounded a trumpet from the top of the tree. Faster than I can tell you about it, milk began to spurt from one part of the fountain while wine and beer poured out of the snakes' mouths.

Of course, this great great great great grandfather of the automated vending machine was operated by well-hidden servants. One servant played the trumpet; others pumped the milk and wine and beer up into the serpents' mouths.

There are other stories that show how excited our ancestors were with gadgets that did not require human effort.

According to the Finnish sagas, there was a great hero whose ship needed no man to set the course. The ship understood the commander's orders and followed the requested course without the help of a human hand. As you have probably heard, trains have now been developed that run by instructions from a computer. The Finnish saga was just a little ahead of its time.

In a medieval legend you may read about a great bronze head that was placed in a giant's castle. This bronze head had a remarkable superhuman gift—it could answer any question you might ask about the past, the present, or the future. You have surely heard of the amount of information that can now be stored inside a computer's "brain." These bits of information can be used to recall the past—for example, how much money you have spent out of your checking account at the bank. The information can also be used to predict, on the basis of mathematical formulas, facts about the future.

As you can easily see, some of the old dreams, legends, and stories have become real today.

In ancient times there was a legend about a bronze head that could answer questions of the past, present, and future. Here is the legend come true—the computer brain.

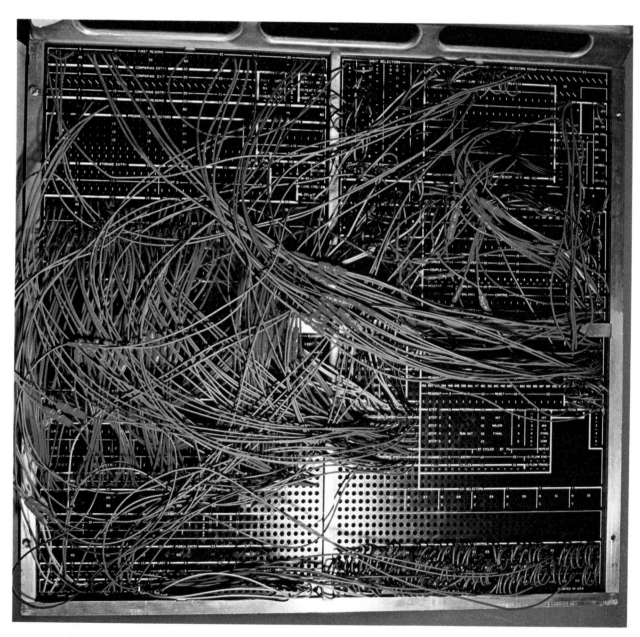

118

AT HOME WITH AUTOMATION

When your great grandmother was a little girl, there was a lot more hard work to do around the house than there is now. In those long ago times, before everyone had such luxuries as electricity, self-operating furnaces, and huge refrigerators, people simply had to work harder to do everything around the house.

In the morning your great grandmother or her parents probably had to get up bright and early to stir up the fire for a little warmth. The next stop would be the stove, which burned coal or wood. The stove had to be heated so that breakfast could be cooked and the bread baked. During the harvest season jams, jellies, and all kinds of preserves were cooked at home on top of that same stove. While the women were doing their work inside, the men were milking the cows, feeding the chickens, and performing a thousand other jobs that had to be done just to stay alive.

Back in the kitchen your great grandmother might have helped churn the butter and wash the clothes—a big job in the days before washing machines—and then iron them with a clumsy coal-burning iron that was very hard to use.

All through the day, as you can easily imagine, there was work to be done. There was little time to sit down and daydream, let alone listen to the radio or watch television—all of which were still unheard-of at that time.

Now, with the help of a thousand different machines, housework has been made so simple that it can almost be done by pushing some buttons. Push the button and an electric stove heats up. Open your refrigerator and pull out a bottle of milk or a stick of butter—products of mass produc-

119

tion and mass distribution. Your freezer can also produce such nearly automatic marvels as a completely cooked dinner that only needs to be heated in the oven. Or perhaps you'd rather have some ice cream that you did not have to make in a hand-cranked machine as your great grandmother did.

If we leave the kitchen and its electrically operated can openers, quick-cooking radiant-heat ovens, automatic dishwashers, and electric mixers, we shall find more miracles of automation elsewhere in the house.

In the laundry you may find a washing machine that requires nothing from you except a cup of soap and the push of a button or two. It does all the hard work of scrubbing, bleaching, and rinsing by itself —your own friendly, time-saving golem! When the laundry is done, all you have to do is throw it in a dryer, which does everything but fold and sort the clothes for you. Maybe you can design a robot that does those jobs.

Probably your house is cool in the summer and cozily warm in the winter. And, if you are like me, you just enjoy the warmth and don't think too much about how it came to be so cozy. The secret of your home heating system is in the thermostat. The thermostat reacts to changes in room temperature. If it gets cooler or warmer than the thermostat setting says it should be, a breaker arm curls or uncurls, closing or opening the switch that turns the furnace on or off. Automation keeps your house comfortable.

AUTOMATION—WHAT IT IS AND HOW IT WORKS

Now that we have seen how men struggled to make life a little easier for themselves in stories and in fact, let's look at one important result—automation.

First of all I must tell you that automation is a word with many different definitions. Most people agree that automation describes any machine or process that is self-regulating and self-controlling. In other words, your furnace is an example of an automated machine because it is self-regulating and self-controlling.

The great benefit of automation, wherever it is found, from your basement to a huge factory, is that it saves men labor. But automation does not mean that men do not have to work anymore. That day is still far, far off. It takes people to design automated machinery and processes. It takes people to run them and to keep them working. And there is a lot more to it than just pushing buttons. Men's brains are needed to make automation work.

Maybe you are wondering where automation can be put to work. The experts tell me that you can automate almost any process that can be broken down into small steps that are repeated over and over again. But it must be less expensive to build the machines than to use human labor before people will consider automating a process like an automobile assembly line or even sorting cards.

Automating a machine or a process requires three big steps. First, you need a machine to do the job. Second, you need some sort of control to discover and measure errors the machine might make.

A housewife's dream—a kitchen staffed (up to a point) by robots. A robot controls the heat on the burners and in the ovens. It turns the ovens on and off. A robot keeps the refrigerator cold and frost free. It supplies the family with ice. Another robot washes and dries the dishes. A robot in the sink chews up the garbage. And all this while, other robots are keeping the house warm in the winter and cool in the summer.

The people of Mexico City are very proud of their subway system. Here we see the very heart of the system —the control panel that directs the movements of all trains.

Third, you need a feedback system that would correct the error. The furnace, the thermostat, and the breaker arm represent these three steps.

Sounds pretty simple doesn't it? Well, it is and it isn't. Obviously if it were as simple as it sounds people would have been using automation for much longer than they have. Automation is an example of a great idea (like flying) that was talked about long before the right machinery to carry out the idea was invented. In this case the missing machines were instruments that could measure error automatically and other instruments that could correct the error. Our famous furnace operates on a fairly simple electric switch. It takes a far more complicated device to direct a cutting tool to make an adjustment of a fraction of an inch. The development of electronic devices made it possible to measure such small amounts. It also made

it possible to correct tiny but very important errors.

The next step was the development of very complicated computers that could be used to direct the automation of a machine or process. These computers have been developed mainly since the end of World War II in 1945.

The computer usually holds a "program" of step-by-step directions on tape. The tape goes into an electronic machine that "reads" the tape and actually operates the motors that move the tool into position for work.

You may be wondering where these 21st century machines are working. I knew you'd be asking, so I found out the answer. Automated machinery is now used to make automobile parts, to refine oil, to run electric power plants, and to roll steel bars into sheets. And that's just the beginning of the list.